# Castile Soapmaking
## The Smart Guide to Making Castile Soap

— Anne L. Watson —

For centuries, the name Castile has been associated with the highest quality in soap. But Castile—made from olive oil, traditionally in factories—has proven hard to translate to craft soapmaking. It has earned a reputation as difficult to make, slow to cure, and lacking in rich lather.

Until now.

Anne L. Watson, author of *Smart Soapmaking*, continues her soapmaking revolution with the first practical book on making Castile soap at home. With the secrets revealed in this advanced guide, you'll be making lovely, quick-curing, lather-rich Castile with no trouble at all.

*"Olive Tree," from* The Grocer's Encyclopedia, *by Artemas Ward, 1911*

# Castile Soapmaking

The Smart Guide to Making
Castile Soap
OR
How to Make Bar Soaps From Olive Oil
With Less Trouble and Better Results

Anne L. Watson

Shepard Publications
Bellingham, Washington

Text and photos copyright © 2015, 2016, 2022, 2024 by Anne L. Watson
Image restorations copyright © 2015, 2016 by Shepard Publications
Proofer photo copyright © 2021 by Mark Shepard
Permission is granted to copy or reprint portions for any noncommercial use, except they may not be posted online without permission.

Special thanks to The Curious Soapmaker for information about traditional Castile soapmaking.

Version 2.1

For updates, more resources, and
personal answers to your questions,
visit Anne's Soapmaking Page at

**www.annelwatson.com/soapmaking**

# Contents

| | |
|---|---|
| Getting Started | 5 |
|    Facts and Myths About Castile | |
| The Keys to Castile | 9 |
|    Moving It from Factory to Kitchen | |
| What Do I Put Into It? | 16 |
|    The Ingredients of Castile | |
| What Do I Use to Make It? | 21 |
|    Gathering the Equipment You Need | |
|    **Anne's Classic Castile** | 24 |
| Step-by-Step Castile Soapmaking | 25 |
|    From Prep to Cleanup and Beyond | |
| More Recipes! | 31 |
|    Different Castile Soaps You Can Try | |
|    **Milk Castile** | 33 |
|    **Herbal Castile** | 34 |
|    **Oatmeal Castile** | 35 |
|    **Cleansing Castile** | 36 |
|    **Gardener's Lemon Poppy Seed Castile** | 37 |
|    **Castor Castile** | 38 |
|    **Castor Coconut Castile** | 39 |
|    **Tropical Castile** | 40 |
| Why? Why? Why? | 42 |
|    Frequently Asked Questions | |
| Where to Find More | 45 |

*Boiling room in a 19th-century Marseille soap factory, from* Les merveilles de l'industrie (Marvels of Industry), *by Louis Figuier, 1873–1877*

# Getting Started
## Facts and Myths About Castile

Castile soap is a soap made from olive oil, sometimes with other plant fats mixed in. It takes its name from the Castile region of Spain, where it was made. But similar soap has been linked to other places where olive oil was plentiful, such as Crete, Nablus, Damascus, Aleppo, and Marseille.

There are romantic stories about the soap's origins—stories involving queens, crusaders, and the Silk Road—but little or no reliable information. Plant oil soaps, though, were probably developed in the Middle East in medieval times to meet religious objections to the use of animal fats. Castile soap itself is thought to have been inspired by Aleppo soap from Syria, but it omitted that soap's laurel berry oil, which was not easily available in Spain.

Unlike Marseille soap from France, Castile soap has never been legally regulated for content. But it was originally a solid soap made exclusively from olive oil. Hot processing was the only soapmaking method in earlier times—in fact, soapmakers were called "soap boilers," and their patron saint, St. Florian, was shared with firefighters.

Going by histories and old pictures, soaps like Castile were produced in factories, using unsophisticated equipment and apparently no safety precautions at all. There seems to be no record of Castile soap being made at home. Compared with cottage soap, which was made with reclaimed kitchen grease, Castile was definitely a luxury item.

Castile soap is regarded by many as the pinnacle of the soapmaker's craft. It's also believed to be difficult to make, and especially difficult to make well by a small-scale soapmaker.

It's thought to need lengthy mixing. *And* to need lengthy aging, with some sources recommending a year or more. *And* to have poor lather, or even slimy lather.

These are all myths, based on the trouble that craft soapmakers have had in adapting what was originally a factory process. But making quality Castile soap on a small scale is not only possible, it's even not so difficult. It's just different.

So, now, let's explore the differences and see how to make perfect Castile soap—traditional or with variations—with little trouble at all.

# IMPORTANT!

Since Castile is a specialty soap, this book assumes you already have some experience in craft soapmaking. If that's not true, please set this one aside for a while and read my book *Smart Soapmaking*. That will give you all the background you need to make soap and do it safely.

*Portrait of Saint Florian, patron saint of firefighters and soap boilers, by Francesco del Cossa, c. 1473*

# The Keys to Castile
## Moving It from Factory to Kitchen

I have to admit, how to translate the traditional hot process mass production of Castile soap in factories to a workable method for craft soapmaking was puzzling at first. With 100% olive oil, my usual cold processing gave me a soap that needed curing for a year or more—and after that long a wait, a couple of my batches had no more lather than rocks do. Even more frustrating, I couldn't think what I'd done wrong on those batches.

Problems I'd had myself or heard about from other soapmakers were consistently of several kinds: The soap may take very long to saponify. It may not be hard enough for many uses. It may lather poorly or even have slimy lather, rather like egg white.

Now the good news: Each of those problems has a solution. Even a 100% olive oil soap can be made to saponify quickly, cure quickly to a good hardness, and lather beautifully. And with slight recipe changes, you may get even better results.

## Mixing Time

Here are the tricks I've learned for shortening mixing time and speeding up saponification. But don't use all of them together, or the soap is likely to set too quickly!

**Equipment.** First off, don't try hand-stirring Castile soap—it can take hours! And though a stick blender is essential, not all stick blenders work well, either. I've made Castile with a cheap stick blender and with a good one. With the cheap one, saponification took twenty minutes to half an hour. With the more powerful one? Maybe five minutes, and sometimes much less.

**Temperature.** I've made batches of Castile with oil at room temperature, and others with oil warmed to about 100°F (38°C). Mixing time was always shorter with warmed oil.

**Accelerants.** If you like particular scents or other additives that accelerate saponification, Castile is the perfect soap to use them in!

**Soap gratings.** Since soap itself is an emulsifier, adding a little grated soap to a recipe shortens mixing time. (This can be especially helpful if you insist on hand-stirring!)

In my one experiment with soap gratings, I added finely grated Castile soap to the water and stirred gently till it dissolved before adding the lye. This gave me a lye solution that was opaque and contained granules—but I stirred it long enough to be satisfied that the granules were soap rather than lye. Still, if you try this method, I encourage you to test the finished soap thoroughly with pH paper for any remaining lye specks.

## Hardness and Curing Time

Olive oil soaps were originally hot processed—"cooked," as you might say—and that's really the key to producing hard soap in a reasonable time.

For my Castile soaps, I use a modified form of Cold Process–Oven Process, or CPOP. I've mostly used a portable roaster oven—not a *toaster* oven!—preheating it to about 110°F (43°C) and setting my filled soap mold in it for six to eight hours. The ideal length of time seems to depend on what's in the soap. I recommend the longer time for 100% olive oil.

*Roaster oven*

I've also used a regular oven at 150°F (66°C) for one hour. With this method, I turned off the oven at the end of the cook time but left it closed till it cooled completely—usually overnight.

Other warming devices can do as well. If you prefer an Instant Pot or slow cooker or double boiler or something else, it should work for Castile as long as your mold will fit and the device maintains a good temperature.

Another fine option—not available when I first worked on this book—is the Brød & Taylor Folding Proofer. It's very roomy and can easily be set to any temperature up to 120°F (49°C). Because it warms only gradually, you may have to add an hour or so to your heating time.

After hot processing like this, your Castile soap should cure to good hardness,

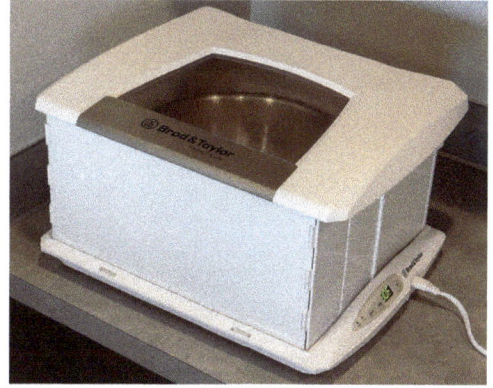
*Brød & Taylor Folding Proofer*

CASTILE SOAPMAKING     11

and in no longer time than you expect with other soaps. As usual, you'll be able to speed this up by storing the soap somewhere warm, dry, and well ventilated.

Of course, how long to let the soap harden is a matter of judgment. If you're using it in the bath or selling it, you'll want to let as much moisture evaporate as possible. If you're using it as hand soap and also have good soap savers, you may be happy with a curing time of a week or two.

Traditionally, at least some olive oil soaps were made with salt water, and some soapmakers believe salt helps these soaps harden faster. Though I normally add salt myself, I can't say I've noticed a big difference between soaps with salt and those without. So, I consider it optional.

Other additives that are commonly tried to improve hardness include sodium lactate, stearic acid, and beeswax. But in my experience, these all reduce lather enough that I consider them poor choices for Castile.

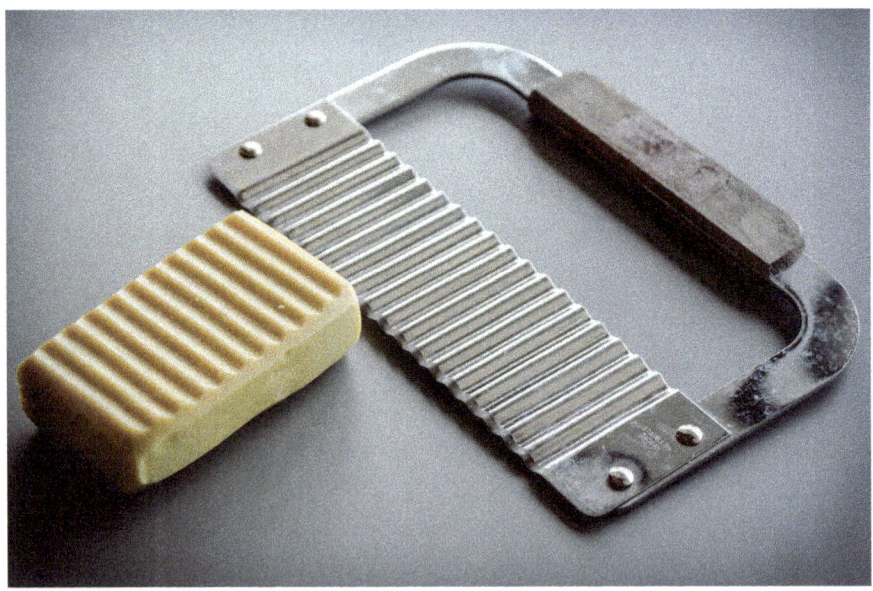

*Crinkle cutter*

# Lather

Finally, here are ways to improve the lather of Castile soap.

**Equipment.** When slicing the soap, use a crinkle cutter. The effect is to increase the surface area of the soap, providing more lather while the crinkles last—which is longer than you might expect.

**Lye.** Most important of all is a small change in the lye. When making bar soap, the lye is generally 100% sodium hydroxide. But replacing just 5% of that with potassium hydroxide will greatly improve the lather of Castile. That's because soap made with potassium hydroxide is more soluble in water—which is one reason it's used for liquid soap. Of course, this also means your Castile will likely not be as hard, even after aging. It's a tradeoff—better lather versus hardness.

This lye replacement is not a one-to-one substitution. Because of slightly different reactions, it takes more potassium hydroxide to react with the same amount of fat. For those of you creating or modifying recipes yourself, I'll go over the calculation in my chapter on ingredients.

**Fats.** You can formulate the soap with small amounts of fats that produce bubbly lather. Check hardness, though, because this may also give you softer soap.

**Additives.** Ingredients with sugars or carbohydrates will boost bubbly lather.

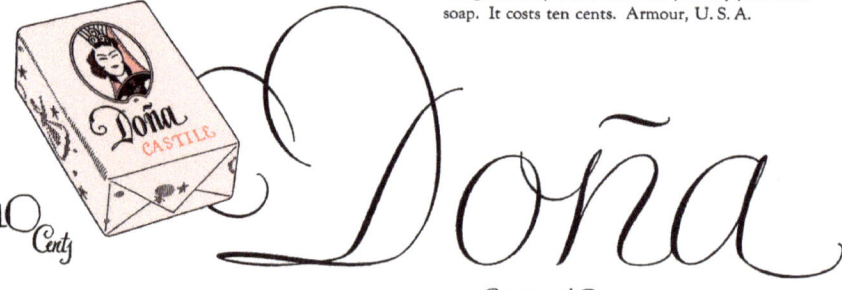

Two-page ad for Doña Castile soap in The Saturday Evening Post, *March 26, 1927,* with art by Ty Mahon

# What Do I Put Into It?
## The Ingredients of Castile

Now let's look closely at what goes into Castile soap.

**Fat**

For a purist, only a 100% olive oil soap would be called Castile. But there's no legal definition, and you'll find the word on labels of commercial soap with under 100% or even under 50%. Most serious craft soapmakers, though, would agree that a soap called Castile should be at least 80% olive oil.

I get a fair number of questions about what kind of olive oil to use. My answer is always, unless the soap's color is important, use the cheapest. Many brands of extra virgin olive oil are adulterated with other oils—and even when they're not, good olive oil for cooking isn't what you need for soapmaking. The cheaper oil has less olive character and may be more acidic, which helps it combine with lye. Save the good olive oil for salad dressing.

If you don't want your soap to be tan or dull green, choose light olive oil, which is lighter in color as well as in taste. Unless you're adding other fats or a darkening scent, olive oil will be your only ingredient with any color, so you can count on about that same color in your soap.

When other fats are added, they're normally ones that improve lather and speed up mixing and curing times—fats like coconut oil and palm kernel oil. Castile with other fats added is sometimes playfully called Bastille.

**Liquid**

Traditionally, water is the liquid for Castile. My primary recipe uses water, but I've tried other liquids as well, some more successfully than others. With any nontraditional liquid, I'd suggest first experimenting with small batches.

**Lye**

Like other craft soapmakers, I've learned to make bar soap with sodium hydroxide, liquid soap with potassium hydroxide. I was surprised to find out that at least one old method of making Castile uses *both* kinds of lye. (Thanks to The Curious Soapmaker for this tip!) Since potassium hydroxide produces a soap more soluble in water, including it improves lather. But including too much will make soap that's too soft.

You can get a good balance by replacing just 5% of the sodium hydroxide with potassium hydroxide. As I mentioned before, you cannot just substitute one lye for an equal amount of the other—but the needed calculation isn't hard. Here's how to figure it, if you're modifying a Castile recipe or creating one on your own:

1. Start with the amount of lye you would need if using 100% sodium hydroxide. Get this amount from the recipe you're modifying, or figure it for a new recipe with a lye calculator. You can work in either ounces or grams, but I recommend grams, as it's a more precise measure.

2. Multiply that original amount of sodium hydroxide by .95. This will be the amount of sodium hydroxide to use in the new formulation.

3. Starting again from the *original* amount of sodium hydroxide, multiply by .07. This is the amount of potassium hydroxide to use. (This is much simpler than other calculations you might

have seen for this substitution, because I've merged two steps and rounded slightly. The difference in results is too small to matter.)

To make sure this is clear, let's look at an example. Say you have a recipe for Castile soap that calls for 100 grams of sodium hydroxide, if used alone. You would take that 100 grams and multiply it by .95. This would give you 95 grams of sodium hydroxide for the new formulation.

100 grams × .95 = 95 grams

Going back to the original 100 grams, you would multiply it again, but this time by .07. This would give you 7 grams of potassium hydroxide.

100 grams × .07 = 7 grams

So, the new formulation would have 95 grams of sodium hydroxide and 7 grams of potassium hydroxide. The total amount of lye will have increased just slightly—in this case, by 2 grams.

95 grams + 7 grams = 102 grams

For those of you who like math and are comfortable thinking in percentages, you could instead describe it this way: Use 95% of the original amount of sodium hydroxide. Then replace the remaining 5% with potassium hydroxide, but increase the amount by 40%. From our example:

100 grams × 95% = 95 grams

100 grams × 5% = 5 grams

5 grams + 40% = 7 grams

The increase in total lye will be 2%. You can use this to check your calculation, figuring the increase in grams and adding it to the original amount of lye. Ignoring slight differences from rounding, the sum should equal the total lye in the new formulation. Returning once more to our example:

100 grams × 2% = 2 grams

2 grams + 100 grams = 102 grams

## Additives

Sugar, salt, and baking soda are additives that may improve the properties of Castile. Sugar—1 to 1½ teaspoons for each pound of fat—will increase bubbly lather. Salt (non-iodized) may increase hardness—though as I said, I haven't seen much difference myself. Baking soda increases bubbly lather and makes the soap more cleansing. Any of these additives should be dissolved in the liquid before adding lye.

Make sure that any color or scent you add can stand up to prolonged heat. If you're not sure, ask your vendor.

Since Castile doesn't set especially quickly, I wondered whether abrasive additives like poppy seeds or dried orange peel would sink to the bottom. In practice, that didn't happen.

*Circus Time Castile clown soap for children, made and hand painted in Austria*

# What Do I Use to Make It?
## Gathering the Equipment You Need

To make Castile soap with my recipes and method, you'll need the following equipment.

- Safety equipment—gloves, goggles, apron, and solid shoes.
- Digital scale, weighing grams or tenths of an ounce.
- Oven thermometer.
- Soup pot or other large pot.
- Large microwave-safe bowl or glass measuring pitcher. I use a four-quart glass batter bowl.
- Bowl, glass measuring pitcher, or stainless steel pan for water and the lye solution. I use the stainless steel top of a double boiler. The curved bottom eliminates corners, which helps with even mixing.
- Two small containers for sodium hydroxide and potassium hydroxide. I use small mason jars.
- Small containers for scent, color, or other additives in the recipe.
- Stick blender. Don't skimp on this one, because a more powerful blender will radically shorten your mixing time.
- Long-handled spoon—steel, stainless steel, or plastic.
- Spatula—rubber or silicone.
- A plate or other dish as a utensil rest. I use a pottery quiche pan. It's big enough for several utensils, and the raised edge ensures that no liquid will run over.
- Covered soap mold, wood or silicone. Cardboard or plastic molds will *not* withstand the needed heat. Mine is a silicone

log mold. It didn't come with its own cover, so I use a silicone universal lid. For my recipes, the mold must hold about 5 cups (1.2 liters). In the U.S., this size is called two-pound.

- Oven or roaster oven, or a different warming device. Whatever you use, make sure you can properly vent any fumes while the soap is cooking.

If you're buying a roaster oven for soapmaking, see if you can find one with a glass window in the lid. But these tend to be smaller, so also make sure your soap mold will fit.

The dial thermostats on most roaster ovens don't have markings for the low temperatures I recommend—100°F–110°F (38°C–43°C). But you can usually get these temperatures by turning the dial to the unmarked area and experimenting. Once the oven is at the temperature you want, you can place a bit of masking tape next to the dial and mark the position with a pen.

- pH papers that read at least between the values of 7 and 14 (highly recommended).
- Crinkle cutter (optional).
- Vegetable peeler (optional).

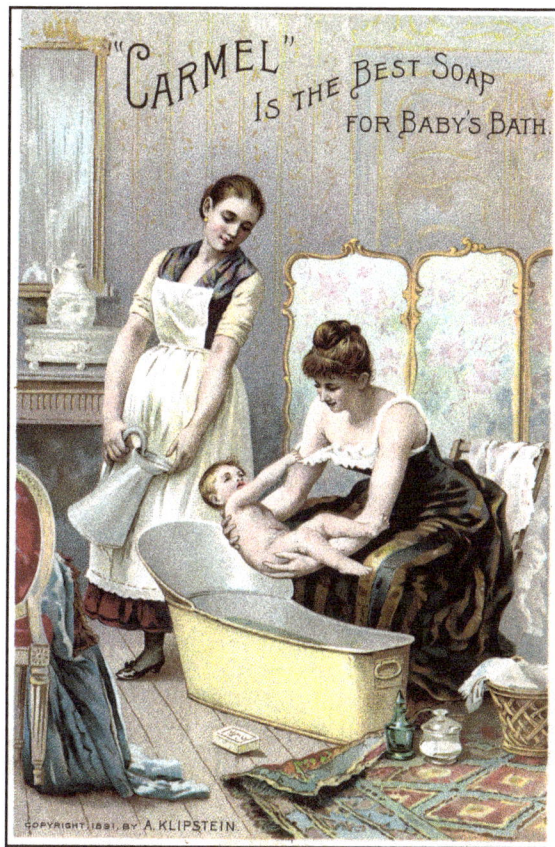

*Trade card for Carmel Soap, front and back, 1891*

At the foot of Mt. Carmel, a Mission Society has taken advantage of the superior **OLIVE OIL** made in Palestine, to support itself by the manufacture of an exceptionally fine Olive Oil Toilet Soap, which they ship direct to their agent, A. KLIPSTEIN, 122 Pearl Street, New York. Both maker and importer **GUARANTEE** the quality. It has been favorably known in America for many years as

### CARMEL SOAP.

It contains no adulteration, is not artificially perfumed, and depends for popular favor on the simple fact of its absolute purity.

Possessing the emollient properties of Olive Oil, it is unsurpassed for the toilet and bath, and superior to all other soaps for the teeth and hair.

As a **NURSERY SOAP** it has no equal, being, in fact, simply the **PUREST FORM** of **CASTILE SOAP**, and being pressed into cakes is **MORE CONVENIENT** to use and **MORE ECONOMICAL** than the old unreliable bar form of Castile Soap.

FOR SALE BY

### BIBO BROS. & CO
San Francisco, Cal

# Anne's Classic Castile

Here is the recipe I recommend for your first efforts at Castile soapmaking. This soap takes about two weeks to cure enough to have excellent thick creamy-bubbly lather.

It's handy to copy this recipe so you don't have to flip pages back and forth as you work through the instructions.

   30 ounces (850 grams) olive oil
   9 ounces (255 grams) distilled water
   1 teaspoon non-iodized salt (optional)
   1 tablespoon sugar (optional)
   3.7 ounces (104 grams) sodium hydroxide
   .3 ounce (8 grams) potassium hydroxide

**Before proceeding, read the following pages thoroughly to understand the method!**

# Step-by-Step Castile Soapmaking
## From Prep to Cleanup and Beyond

Here I'll describe how to make my basic Castile soap by the method called Cold Process–Oven Process, or CPOP. I find it to be the best of the hot processes—quick, comparatively safe, and not messy. If you prefer another hot process, though, you can adapt these instructions to suit it. CPOP does have one disadvantage: Scent is likelier to fade, because it's added before cooking.

Don't forget safety. Protect yourself from the slightest contact with the lye or soap mixture at all times. From the moment you open a container of lye until cleanup is complete, you must wear rubber gloves, goggles, protective clothing, and solid shoes. Watch your hands and your work carefully as you weigh and add the lye. Make sure there is no spillage. If there is, clean it up at once.

Make sure your workspace is well ventilated and you avoid inhaling lye fumes. I open windows and also work under my range hood with the vent fan on high. When you're stirring the lye solution, keep the container far from your face.

For hot processes like CPOP, there's an extra safety requirement you may not be aware of: Protect yourself and other household members from fumes while the soap is cooking. These fumes can spread through your home to irritate your lungs even when you're nowhere near the soap. You might not notice the effect from a single batch, but as you make more, it can creep up on you.

Here again, ventilation is key. With a typical range or stove, you can just turn the hood fan on high. A roaster oven could be placed under the same hood fan or even in a sheltered spot outside. Built-in standalone ovens are *not* vented to the outside, so if you use one, you'll need to open windows or doors.

## Making the Soap

1. Preheat your oven or other warming device. With a roaster oven, set it to Warm or around 100°F–110°F (38°C–43°C). With an ordinary baking oven, use its lowest temperature, which will probably be between 150°F and 170°F (66°C and 77°C).

2. Weigh the olive oil into the microwave-safe container. Warm it to about 110°F (43°C). Then transfer it to your soup pot.

3. Weigh the water into your water container.

4. Add the sugar and salt if you're using them. Stir until they dissolve *completely*.

5. If you haven't already, put on gloves, goggles, and other protective clothing.

6. Weigh the sodium hydroxide and potassium hydroxide into separate containers.

7. Add the sodium hydroxide and potassium hydroxide to the water and stir well until fully dissolved. Always add lye to water, NEVER the other way around.

8. Add the lye solution to the oil in the soup pot. Stir briefly but well with your long-handled spoon.

9. Mix with the stick blender. Move it through the mixture so everything gets mixed thoroughly.

You'll soon see changes in the mixture. Originally oily and transparent, it will become creamy and opaque. The surface, which was shiny at first, will become duller, and the oily ring at the edge of the mixture's surface—right where it meets the wall of the pot—will shrink and all but disappear.

Next you'll notice the mixture thickening and getting smoother. It will come to resemble thick eggnog or very thin pudding. At this point, you can stop blending, because the saponification that produces soap can continue without further mixing. You might call this "the point of no return." (You *don't* have to keep mixing long enough to see "trace," as other instructions might call for.)

Besides these visual signs, you can get a feel for the thickness by turning off the blender and briefly stirring with it like a spoon. With a weaker blender, you can even *hear* the difference, as the thickening slows down the blade, causing the sound of the motor to drop in pitch.

After finishing with the stick blender, I remove it and use a rubber spatula to stir carefully at the bottom of the pot, including the edge. This helps to make sure everything is mixed thoroughly.

10. Pour the soap mixture into your mold. Then cover the mold and put it in your preheated oven or other device.

11. Clean up *with your gloves and goggles still on*. Wash all containers and utensils carefully. If you use a dishwasher, wash your utensils once by hand before loading them. (If you don't, your dishwasher will probably run over.) If you're washing *only* by hand, wash twice. Pay special attention to handles and the outer lip of the pot. Wipe down your work surfaces with damp paper towels, then with your usual cleaning solution.

Finally, wash your gloves *with your hands still inside.*

*Now* take off your gloves and goggles.

12. How long you cook the soap will depend on the temperature of your oven or other device. For example, with a roaster oven set to 100°F–110°F (38°C–43°C), leave it about eight hours. With an ordinary baking oven at 150°F–170°F (66°C–77°C), turn it off after an hour, but let it return to room temperature with the mold still inside. For temperatures in between, figure accordingly.

13. Take out the mold and let it stand a few more hours at room temperature to let the soap cool and solidify. Or with a baking oven, you can just turn off the oven in the evening and let the mold sit in it overnight.

## Removal and Testing

When the mold is cool to the touch, remove the soap, again with gloves on. Then let it sit a few more hours to let the entire block come to room temperature.

At this point, it shouldn't be caustic, but keep your gloves on while you test that. Put a little distilled water on the soap's surface, scrub it around to make a paste, then push a pH strip into the paste. If the strip shows anything in the range of 7 to 10, the soap is fine. The exact pH reading doesn't matter—the strips aren't all that accurate anyway. But they *will* let you know if your soap is in a safe range.

It's very unlikely that soap you've cooked will give a high pH reading. But in the event the pH strip reads 11 or 12, let the soap sit a few days and test it again—it may just need more time. If your reading is above 12, don't use the soap and don't touch it without gloves. Sometimes a very high pH does slowly decrease till the soap is usable. More often, though, the soap needs to be discarded or rebatched.

If the outer surface tests OK, slice the block in half and look at the cut surfaces. Your soap should have a texture that's fairly smooth and regular, with a consistency like cheese. It may be slightly sticky on the cut edges, and there may be a small difference in texture or color between the cut faces and the outer surface of the block—something like a rind covering a soft cheese. This is normal.

Test one of the cut surfaces with a pH strip. Also test anything that looks unusual—a shiny patch, a light spot, anything that stands out from the rest. Once in a long while, you may get a high reading on something that looks "off." When that happens to me, I discard or rebatch the entire block.

If it all tests OK, you're home free.

## Cutting and Curing

After testing the soap successfully, remove your gloves and finish slicing the soap into bars. I cut Castile with a crinkle cutter, because a wavy surface makes more lather. If you like, you can trim the sides of the bars to make them neater. You can also smooth the edges by beveling them with a vegetable peeler.

With hot processing, my recipes with 100% olive oil give usable results with a curing time much shorter than they'd need with cold processing—usually no more than a week or two. But you might want to let the soap dry and cure longer, for increased hardness and better lather.

How can you be sure the soap is dry enough? Just try a bar. If it gets used up too fast or gets gooey, or if the lather is poor, that soap needs more time. The longer the bars dry—up to a couple of months or so—the harder they'll be and the longer they'll last in use.

*Santa's Reindeer Castile animal soap for children, made by Lightfoot soap company, USA*

# More Recipes!
## Different Castile Soaps You Can Try

You can make variations on traditional Castile by using different liquids or additives. You can also change its character by substituting different fats. "Bastille" is the tongue-in-cheek nickname that soapmakers give to soaps that are not 100% olive oil but generally at least 80%. The preferred substitutes are fats producing more bubbly lather, such as coconut oil and palm kernel oil. These fats also help the soap saponify and cure more quickly.

All my recipes have 30 ounces of fat (850 grams), requiring a soap mold that will hold at least 5 cups (1.2 liters).

For the most part, you should follow the directions I've already given, unless the recipe says something different. But there are two general exceptions:

1. If one of the fats is solid, just melt it and add it to the olive oil, omitting the part about heating the olive oil separately.

2. If a recipe includes castor oil, you might want to lower the cooking temperature or shorten the time to avoid overheating. If the soap gets too hot, the top surface will heave and become irregular. But if this does happen, the problem is only cosmetic, and you can just trim off that edge when cutting the soap.

## Recipe Checking

Before trying a new soap recipe—mine or anyone else's—always check the given amounts of lye and water with a lye calculator to make sure they're correct. Even if the recipe comes from a published book, don't use it till you're sure it's free of error—and that goes double for any recipe you find online.

I've already explained how you can figure the amounts of lye when replacing some sodium hydroxide with potassium hydroxide. When checking a recipe that has both kinds of lye, you'll need to *reverse* that calculation and figure how much sodium hydroxide you would use on its own. Here's how:

1. Take the amount of potassium hydroxide and multiply by .7.
2. Add this to the amount of sodium hydroxide. With a slight bit of rounding, that is how much you would use of sodium hydroxide alone.

Let's go back to our earlier example, which started with 100 grams of sodium hydroxide and wound up with 95 grams of sodium hydroxide and 7 grams of potassium hydroxide. You would first multiply the 7 grams of potassium hydroxide by .7, giving 4.9 grams—which we would round to 5.

7 grams × .7 = 5 grams

Then we'd add that to the 95 grams, giving us 100.

5 grams + 95 grams = 100 grams

Since that was the original amount of lye in the example, we know the replacement amounts are OK. And actually, if you see a difference of a gram or a tenth of an ounce, it would still probably be fine. Such a difference can be caused just by rounding twice—once in the original calculation, and once in reversing it.

# Milk Castile

Buttermilk is a good choice of liquid for Castile soap; so is yogurt diluted by mixing it 50-50 with distilled water. A fermented milk product like one of these will make a lighter soap than one that still has all its milk sugar. Goat milk is fine, too.

This soap will be tan or beige, not white. Although milk soaps are often made with frozen milk to avoid darkening, it's pointless here because the soap is cooked anyway.

- 30 ounces (850 grams) olive oil
- 9 ounces (255 grams) milk
- 1 teaspoon non-iodized salt (optional)
- 1 tablespoon sugar (optional)
- 3.7 ounces (104 grams) sodium hydroxide
- .3 ounce (8 grams) potassium hydroxide

# Herbal Castile

There are many herbs that will give your soap a lovely natural color. But don't mix dried herbs into the soap itself or add them as a topping, because they may turn brown as you cook them, or feel dry and scratchy as you use the soap.

Instead, infuse your olive oil with herbs ahead of time by steeping them in the oil for at least a month in a cool, dark place. To allow for loss in the process, infuse more oil than your recipe needs. For each pound (half kilogram) of oil, add from one-quarter to one cup (about 12 to 48 grams) of dried herbs. I use herbs that are commercially dried, to avoid mold and spoilage. Cover the container tightly. Before use, strain the oil through a fine sieve.

To shorten the steeping time, you can infuse the oil in much the same way you'd make sun tea: Put the oil and herbs into a clear glass jar and set it in the sun for a week or so. Don't use a slow cooker—in my experience, that scorches the oil.

If you're after scent instead of color, use essential oil or fragrance oil instead. Some herb essential oils will accelerate trace—so if you use one that will, omit the sugar and don't warm the oil.

- 30 ounces (850 grams) herb-infused olive oil
- 9 ounces (255 grams) distilled water
- 1 teaspoon non-iodized salt (optional)
- 1 tablespoon sugar (optional)
- 3.7 ounces (104 grams) sodium hydroxide
- .3 ounce (8 grams) potassium hydroxide

# Oatmeal Castile

This is a soothing soap that lathers well. Dissolve the salt and sugar in the oat milk before adding the lye. When you add lye to oat milk, the liquid becomes gelatinous and steamy. Stir until the lye is dissolved and strain through a wire sieve before adding the solution to the oil.

I use homemade oat milk. To make it, combine one-half cup (about 90 grams) rolled oats with 3¼ cups (about three-quarters liter) distilled water. Cover and let stand overnight. In the morning, blend or stick blend till smooth. Strain through a fine sieve or nut milk bag.

If you use commercial oat milk instead, be sure to check the ingredients on the label. If they include sugar or salt, reduce or eliminate that ingredient in the recipe.

Adding rolled oats as a decoration on top may give the soap a nice look, but I advise against it. The oats will get soggy and may also attract insects.

This soap takes me a little longer than most to saponify—about fifteen minutes with a stick blender.

    30 ounces (850 grams) olive oil
    9 ounces (255 grams) oat milk
    1 teaspoon non-iodized salt (optional)
    1 tablespoon sugar (optional)
    3.7 ounces (104 grams) sodium hydroxide
    .3 ounce (8 grams) potassium hydroxide

# Cleansing Castile

This soap is more cleansing and less emollient than most Castile soaps. The baking soda helps produce good bubbly lather. Dissolve the baking soda in the water before adding the lye.

  30 ounces (850 grams) olive oil
  9 ounces (255 grams) distilled water
  2 teaspoons baking soda
  3.7 ounces (104 grams) sodium hydroxide
  .3 ounce (8 grams) potassium hydroxide

# Gardener's Lemon Poppy Seed Castile

This is a gentle scrub soap meant especially for gardeners. I use fragrance oil for this recipe, since citrus essential oils are delicate and probably wouldn't survive cooking. Mix in the poppy seeds and fragrance just before pouring the soap into the mold.

- 30 ounces (850 grams) olive oil
- 9 ounces (255 grams) distilled water
- 1 teaspoon non-iodized salt (optional)
- 1 tablespoon sugar (optional)
- 3.7 ounces (104 grams) sodium hydroxide
- .3 ounce (8 grams) potassium hydroxide
- 1 tablespoon poppy seeds
- 2 ounces (55 grams) fragrance oil, lemon or lemon verbena

# Castor Castile

Don't add sugar to this Bastille soap, because castor oil and sugar both accelerate saponification. For the same reason, don't warm the olive oil or use a trace-accelerating fragrance.

- 27 ounces (765 grams) olive oil
- 3 ounces (85 grams) castor oil
- 9 ounces (255 grams) distilled water
- 1 teaspoon non-iodized salt (optional)
- 3.6 ounces (103 grams) sodium hydroxide
- .3 ounce (8 grams) potassium hydroxide

# Coconut Castor Castile

This Bastille soap lathers extravagantly right away, and with a pale olive oil, the recipe gives you nearly white soap. For this one too, don't warm the olive oil, add sugar, or use a trace-accelerating fragrance—the castor oil speeds up saponification on its own.

    24 ounces (680 grams) olive oil
    4.5 ounces (128 grams) coconut oil
    1.5 ounces (43 grams) castor oil
    9 ounces (255 grams) distilled water
    1 teaspoon non-iodized salt (optional)
    3.8 ounces (108 grams) sodium hydroxide
    .3 ounce (8 grams) potassium hydroxide

# Tropical Castile

Murumuru butter is pressed from the seeds of a tropical palm tree. It is one of the few plant butters that contributes significantly to bubbly lather in soap. It's white, odorless, and easy to work with.

- 24 ounces (680 grams) olive oil
- 3 ounces (85 grams) coconut oil
- 1.5 ounces (43 grams) castor oil
- 1.5 ounces (43 grams) murumuru butter
- 9 ounces (255 grams) distilled water
- 1 teaspoon non-iodized salt (optional)
- 1 tablespoon sugar (optional)
- 3.9 ounces (110 grams) sodium hydroxide
- .3 ounce (8 grams) potassium hydroxide

*Ad for Knight's Castile soap, 1920*

# Why? Why? Why?
## Frequently Asked Questions

*How long should I wait to use my soap?*

Assuming the soap passes its pH test, you could use it right away. But you'll get better lather and harder soap if you let it cure a few weeks.

*What if I want to use different fats than the ones in your Bastille soap recipes?*

If you use different fats, you must recalculate the lye. For best results, use fats with high values of bubbly lather.

*What if I want to make larger or smaller batches than yours?*

You can reduce or increase all the recipe quantities proportionally, just as with a cooking recipe—but of course, you have to be more accurate than if you're making dinner.

*Should I use extra virgin olive oil? What about pomace?*

Extra virgin olive oil is more likely than any other grade to be adulterated with cheaper oils. I guess, if a producer or supplier is going to cheat, they might as well do it for top price!

Pomace, the lowest and formerly cheapest grade of olive oil, is perfect for soapmaking. Unfortunately, demand from soapmakers has driven the price up, so you're paying more for lower quality!

My advice with olive oil is to use the cheapest kind that will work for you. If you want light-colored soap, or if you're using a delicate fragrance, light olive oil will probably be your best choice. But other than that, buy on price.

*Help! My soap won't come out of the mold!*

Put the mold in the freezer for a while—maybe fifteen to twenty minutes to start. The soap will harden and shrink a bit. It will then be much easier to remove.

### Author Online!

For updates, more resources, and personal answers to your questions, visit Anne's Soapmaking Page at

**www.annelwatson.com/soapmaking**

# Where to Find More

**Anne's Soapmaking Page**

Check here for my latest experiments in soapmaking. There's always more to try and to learn!

    www.annelwatson.com/soapmaking

**SoapCalc**

This site is one of the most useful sources of soapmaking information and formula analysis. It's nearly indispensable for designing your own recipes.

    www.soapcalc.net

**The Curious Soapmaker**

A wonderful blog about all things soap, including Castile.

    curious-soapmaker.com

## About the Author

Anne L. Watson is the first author to have introduced modern techniques of home soapmaking and lotionmaking to book readers. She has made soap under the company name Soap Tree, and before her retirement from professional life, she was a historic preservation architecture consultant.

Besides her soap and lotion books, Anne has written practical guides to such topics as cookie molds and housekeeping, along with a number of literary novels and children's books. She and her husband, Aaron Shepard, live in Bellingham, Washington. You can visit her at

**www.annelwatson.com**

# BOOKS BY

# ANNE L. WATSON

 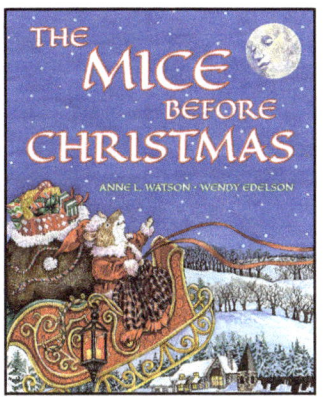 

*and more . . .*

www.ingramcontent.com/pod-product-compliance
Lightning Source LLC
Chambersburg PA
CBHW060855090426
42736CB00023B/3490